THE PRINCIPLE OF:

Love
&
Marriage

THE PRINCIPLE OF:

Love

&

Marriage

OR: HOW TO BE MARRIED "HAPPILY EVER AFTER"

Jim Holtslag

ARPress
ILLUMINATING IDEAS.
EMPOWERING VOICES

ARPress LLC
45 Dan Road Suite 5
Canton MA 02021
Hotline: 1(888) 821-0229
Fax: 1(508) 545-7580

Ordering Information:
Quantity sales. Special discounts are available on quantity purchases by corporations, associations, and others. For details, contact the publisher at the address above.

Printed in the United States of America.

ISBN-13:   Softcover   979-8-89330-695-8
            eBook   979-8-89330-694-1

Library of Congress Control Number: 2024902824

I dedicate this book to Gail; my high school sweetheart, my beloved wife, best friend, mother of my children, Nana to my grandchildren and Lifelong instructor to me In the art of love.

Jim Holtslag

CONTENTS

Introduction

For many years in the late 1980's and all of the 1990's, my wife and I were involved in or led the marriage preparation process in our local church. The process centered around sitting down with the engaged couple, one on one, in our home, and over the course of many hours (spread out over many weeks), would insure that the couple was effectively communicating with each other on all the subjects that should be explored before entering into marriage. It started with the easy subjects, such as family backgrounds and how that can effect expectations and worked up to more sensitive subjects such as expectations for child rearing, finances and sexuality. To facilitate open discussion, my wife and I would bring up anecdotal examples from our own experience, but would emphasize that what works for some people would not necessarily work for others as everyone has different backgrounds and experiences. The important thing was that there was good communication between them.

As a result, we got to know a large number of couples that were planning to be married, on a much more intellectually intimate level than friends that we may have had for years and years. With only one exception in the scores and scores of couples, we found these couples to be very much in love, communicating well on most of the right things, and fully expecting to live happily ever after. I don't know if any of these discussions ever actually helped any of these couples, but I know it helped our own marriage by forcing us to discuss and to understand experiences that we had gone through, in order to relate them to these engaged couples (without getting kicked under the table).

The troublesome part about the whole experience was that, assuming these couples were representative of most young people getting married, why is the chance that these couples will end up in a divorce 40%[1]? Why do almost half of the couples who get married end up getting divorced especially in the first three to five years? These are good people with good intentions seemingly very much in love! What is going wrong?

Even more troublesome to me, is my observation that many people who have not gotten divorced, nor ever expect to, have a marriage that seems better characterized as having developed a mutual tolerance for each other, allowing the conveniences of living together to outweigh the inconveniences. It is fairly rare that you find marriages in which the people will tell you that their marriage is an incredible source of happiness and fulfillment and that it is at the very center of their lives. Why is this? Why does marriage work so well for a small minority, but fail for the majority?

I'm an engineer in both training and disposition. Engineers (and scientists) have one characteristic that sets them apart from the rest of society, at least in its intensity; the need to understand why something happens the way it does. For example, people may observe that the full moon appears bigger at some times than others, or much more overhead than it was just weeks before, this is simply "accepted" by most. It's not that they couldn't figure it out if they wanted to, it's just that they don't feel a need to. It's okay to leave the understanding to someone else. The engineer, on the other hand, needs to know why. This need for understanding is also not a problem for the engineer, since he/she was usually born with this need, hence paid attention in school when explanations were given in the text books and therefore, can easily explain most natural phenomenon that are regularly encountered in life. (The problem is usually for the people around them that have to listen politely to the engineer as he/ she dutifully explains these things to a listener who could usually care less!)

Unlike answering the question of why the moon changes, where you can go to any number of readily available sources that can teach the

---

1   Prof. Scott M. Stanley of Univ. of Denver per Divorcesource.com

basic principles of planetary motion that will allow you to predict where the moon will be and what it will look like tomorrow, next month or ten years from now, I was not aware of any text that would explain to me the principles of marriage that would allow me to understand where my marriage would be tomorrow, next week or ten years from now. So for the past twenty years, this has been an area of interest and study for me.

What I have concluded (and this may come as a shock to you, as it was for me), is that there is a simple, basic principle of marriage that if understood and followed as a guide, can virtually **guarantee** that a marriage **will** be one of those few that is a source of happiness and fulfillment that most other people will never know in their lifetime. The purpose of this book is to explain this basic principle, the problems in applying it, and the expected results if you do apply it to your marriage. This probably sounds incredible at this point, but give it a chance and read on; hopefully you will find that it is so basic and obvious that it must be true!

UNDERSTANDING THE PRINCIPLE

Why is understanding the principle of marriage so important? Let me give you an example. Do you remember the old math story problems you had in school such as: "You need to get somewhere that is 165 miles away. If you drive the 55 mph speed limit, how long will it take you to get there?" The need to understand this principle is like the need to understand the principle behind the story problem. If you understand the basic principle behind the problem, you can figure out what to do to get the correct answer and be completely certain that it is correct. If you don't understand the principle, but you know that sometimes you have to divide one number by another and sometimes you have to multiply them, then you have to **guess** what the right thing to do is. You can base your guess on intuition or whatever worked last time, but more often than not, you will find that you did the wrong thing for that particular situation. This becomes very frustrating and you conclude that you are better off avoiding math problems if you can. Marriage is the same way; because of not understanding the basic principle, many people get frustrated and walk away while others choose to stay married but just avoid the troublesome aspects of the relationship.

This is the situation I found myself in, at least for the first ten years of my marriage. I didn't understand the basic principle, but I always did what I thought was best for a given situation and through some fairly good luck, and perhaps never being handed a really challenging problem, I got it right enough of the time to consider myself "happily married" in a world of unhappy marriages. Now, everything has changed! Having achieved what must be at least a rudimentary understanding of the principle of marriage, I am as confident that my marriage will be a great source of happiness and fulfillment next month or ten years from now as I am that the answer to the above math problem is three hours. I only regret that I did not come to an understanding of the principle of marriage even earlier in the marriage so that I could have avoided the mistakes and risks that come with guessing rather than knowing what to do! If this book can help even one other couple along this line, it will be worth the effort.

This book will **not** tell you what to do or how to act, any more than someone can tell you that in all math problems, you should divide the first number by the second number. All people are different and all situations are unique. What works for one situation will not work for another. However, if you understand and apply the principle yourself, you **will** get the correct outcome. A word of warning though, unlike simple math problems, applying this simple principle to real life situations, does require a level of trust, introspection and self honesty. This won't always be easy, especially at first.

There are just two other observations about this book that I think are important in the way of introduction. First, the principle and ideas presented herein, are not new or original; you have heard it all before in one manner or another. Life is like a big jigsaw puzzle with lots of information just dumped on the table before you. The intention of this book is to help put some of the pieces together so that the big picture becomes clearer. No matter where you are in your relationship, no matter how new or old the relationship is and no matter how good or bad it has been, understanding the principle of marriage can only make it better.

Secondly, a truly great marriage requires a partnership of two like-minded people. If only one is willing to understand and attempt to apply the principle, it is destined to never reach its potential. However, if both are willing to understand and apply the principle, the outcome of a marriage that far exceeds your wildest expectations for happiness and fulfillment is not only likely, it is as certain as math. It will work every time!

CHAPTER 1

Marriage in Trouble

The biggest problem in the United States today is marriage! It's not the economy or ecology or over population, terrorist threats or even the myriad health issues from AIDS to heart disease, the various forms of cancer or the rising cost of health care; I believe its marriage. As bad and as serious as these other things are, none can compare to the personal financial and emotional devastation that is going on, day in and day out in this country due to marriage. There are few people in this country today (if any) that have not or will not suffer significant emotional and/or financial problems as a result of a marriage, be it their own or that of their parents, children or other close friends or relatives. Think of your own experience and that of your family (parents, aunts and uncles, cousins and siblings) along with all of your past and present friends. How many of them have gone through a divorce or are children from a divorced household versus those who have suffered directly from cancer, AIDS, or terrorist attacks? If your experience is anything like mine, the divorces outnumber the other problems by a wide margin.

Don't get me wrong, marriage is supposed to be, and can be, the best thing that ever happens in a person's life; a tremendous source of happiness and growth. The problem is that more times than not, it turns out to be closer to the opposite. And the down side of a bad marriage devastates not only the marriage partners but can poison generations to come through their children and society in general when it becomes the norm. Unfortunately, that is what has happened in this country; bad marriages have not only become the norm but nearly our expectation!

About 40% of all young people getting married in this country today will end up getting divorced[2]. There are probably even some who enter into marriage with the thought that "Well, we'll give it a try, if it doesn't work out, we can always get a divorce." As you will see below, this is not a good plan as the problems and hassles of divorce can be huge:

FINANCIAL PROBLEMS

Consider the financial problems related to divorce. First of all, it is difficult to get an estimate of what a divorce will cost you financially before entering into it because there are so many variables involved. Lawyers typically consider it unethical to even give you an estimate of what your divorce will cost, up front, because many things have the tendency to change as the divorce proceeds and questions of the cost of child custody and responsibility come to light for the first time. Even the most amiable intended divorces seem to grow more hostile as the perceived "pettiness" from the other side creeps into the details of the settlement and are returned in kind. Then there are the family and friends pressuring the contestants to make sure they get a "fair" deal for their side, especially since it is the other side that is <u>really</u> at fault. But this is seldom the perceived result by either side; usually both sides feel they got the bad deal.

The total legal fees related to divorce, can easily cost each side tens of thousands of dollars if it is fairly typical, but if it becomes contentious, can drag on until one side simply runs out of money! Considering that money problems are reportedly the most argued about things in a marriage in the first place, when you now take these tens of thousands of dollars for each side and subtract them from whatever assets the couple had before the divorce, it's no wonder both sides feel they got

---

2   Prof. Scott M. Stanley of Univ. of Denver per Divorcesource.com

cheated when the divorce is finalized; they are both in worse financial shape than before the divorce. The only ones better off are the lawyers and their gain had to come from somewhere!

The legal fees mentioned above, however, are just the tip of the iceberg in the real financial cost of divorce. Divorce usually ends up in both parties moving into an economically more difficult life style. The nice home that was appreciating in value (and for many was the only appreciable financial asset they had) may have to be sold in a temporarily disadvantageous market and replaced by two smaller versions that won't appreciate as fast, or by renting (nothing depreciates faster than a rent receipt). Similarly, other assets such as boats, RV's, cars, etc., may have to be liquidated at a fraction of their worth to you as a result of the settlement. The cost of food will escalate as you find yourself eating out more rather than preparing meals at home for just yourself. Then there is the need for two of every "essential" from toasters to lawnmowers where previously one would suffice. No matter how you cut it, two cannot live separately for what it costs to live together. There will now be two mortgage payments or rent receipts, two sets of electric bills, gas bills, ad infinitum. Even your income tax rate goes up when you are now single. All this extra money must come from somewhere!

Alimony and child support never seem to be reasonable no matter which side you are on. If you are the payer, they often prevent you from living above a meager subsistence level at best. If you are the receiver, it never seems to cover the real cost of living or raising kids and besides, the payer is always delinquent. Babysitting or daycare may become necessary or more frequent because of the lack of a partner to cover certain times of the day, and if kids are older, chauffeuring them to their extracurricular activities will be more difficult to share if your "ex" is even willing to help at all.

There are also many less obvious costs related to divorce. The stress associated with going through a divorce can bring on medical problems to which science is only beginning to understand the linkage. What is obvious is that lethal problems ranging from hypertension to the onset of some cancers can result from these periods of high stress. The medical costs associated with these can be tremendous not only to the victims, but also to society in general as everyone ends up footing the cost of higher healthcare insurance.

Divorce can also result in the need for psychiatric counseling for either the participants or their children because of the change or trauma involved. Often these needs go unmet because of the costs of these long term treatments or the unfortunate stigma society places on the need for this treatment. Unfortunately, the consequences of not getting the treatment can be even higher in terms of dysfunctional behaviors and ruined subsequent lives.

All in all, few people look back on their divorce settlement feeling that it was financially satisfactory to them. Sometimes their expectations begin unreasonably, expecting they would be as well off after the divorce as before. At other times, there really may have been an unfair settlement reached for whatever reason. In any case, the result is that the settlement may be later contested and the whole negative and expensive process starts over again.

EMOTIONAL PROBLEMS

If the only problem that marriages that end in divorce posed for our society was the financial hardship that it brought to its participants, one might rationalize that there are some offsetting financial benefits to society. Divorce keeps a huge part of our legal system in business; and for every asset that had to be liquidated in an untimely manner, someone else may end up with a bargain. Unfortunately, while financial aspects may be the easiest to see, they pale in comparison to the psychological and emotional damage to the participants and society in general. Let's look at some of these problems.

Chronologically, one of the first problems encountered, when divorce is considered, is self esteem: "What are my friends and family going to say and think? It appears that I have failed in a major aspect of my life, either in the initial decision or the subsequent execution, where others have succeeded. How much of that is my fault?" This starts what is usually a long period of anxiety over whether or not divorce is really the best decision. "Will I regret it? Have I tried hard enough to really make it work? Will I lose the love and support of friends and relatives that I truly care about? What will be the effect on our kids? What will it cost? Can I afford it? How will my lifestyle have to change? Where will I live? How ugly will the divorce proceedings get and will I be made out to look like a monster?" These and many more questions will fill many a sleepless night of a person who is considering divorce.

Once the decision has been made and the intent filed, the real problems begin! What was expected to be a rather straightforward "*no fault*" settlement usually gets complicated with unexpected "*pettiness*". The division of assets that should be obvious and straightforward get challenged and you suspect spite or other mind games are going on and want to retaliate. The anxiety and bitterness escalate as you hear second-hand rumors and allegations about what went on in the marriage that you know are completely untrue or are taken out of context; he drank too much, she didn't take care of the house, he was always flirting around, she was a clothes horse, and so on and so forth.

If there are children involved, there is a whole other level of problems and anxieties to have to deal with! Who will have custody? What are the visitation hassles going to be? What will be the effect on the children psychologically? When the children are with the "ex", what kind of negative things will they be told about me? Will they end up hating me? Will they be safe and properly cared for at all times? How will they suffer from growing up in a single parent environment. How will the lack of a good marriage role model affect the children's chances of having a good marriage themselves? On the other hand, how do these concerns compare to the psychological damage that can result from living in a family that is filled with arguing, strife and the other dysfunctionalities that are found in most marriages "on the rocks"?

Finally, if I ever want to marry again, what kind of problems will this divorce present legally or otherwise? If I am Catholic, will I be prevented from marrying in my church? Can I get an annulment? What will happen when the "ex" and my new spouse meet? Will the baggage from the first marriage impact the second?

As daunting as these considerations are, most people considering divorce still find this to be the better option as opposed to staying in the current relationship. This gives you some feeling for how bad it is to be in a bad marriage!

NON-DIVORCE MARRIAGES

Recognizing that nearly half of all marriages will end up in divorce, how about the rest? I've never seen statistics, but my perception is that the majority of those marriages that are not headed for divorce are not the fairytale "lived happily ever after" kind either, but may better be described as two people still living together because it's better than the alternative. Certainly there is a whole spectrum in this category of how good or how bad these non-divorce headed marriages may be, but typically are based on meeting some combinations of needs such as security (financial or emotional),companionship, convenience, appearances, "for the kids", or other needs that outweigh the hassles of living alone or getting a divorce.

On the bad end of the spectrum, there are marriages that should be terminated based on the pain and suffering that is permeating the participants (and their children, if there are any), but something is preventing it. That something could be intimidation that is often connected with situations of abuse in which one partner is afraid that any attempt to leave or terminate the marriage will result in lethal retaliation against themselves or other family members. Another somewhat common reason that bad marriages don't end up in divorce is religious convictions that marriages should never be terminated, once entered into, regardless of how dysfunctional they have become. If there are children involved, unfortunately, growing up in a really dysfunctional family may scar them for life.

Somewhat further up the scale are a large group of marriages, that I'll call amiable marriages, that are based on meeting some internal needs of the participants, other than love. These needs can range from very simple ones like financial security or the desire to have children, to very complicated emotional needs that the participants themselves may not be fully aware of. As long as the needs are met, the marriage is satisfactory to them. Also in this group, are marriages of convenience which, although they did not necessarily start out this way, for all intent and purpose, have evolved into what might best be described as "married singles". Each person has their own circle of friends, hobbies and interests; they just co-habit the same house and bed. They may even take separate vacations. I suspect in most of these marriages, the subject of divorce never even comes up. If you asked these people if they love each other, the honest answer would be "of course . . . , I guess so", but, in fact, that subject never comes up, and the words are never spoken.

Just because these marriages don't end up in divorce, doesn't mean that the emotional and psychological damage they do to themselves and people around them is inconsequential! Certainly those marriages that are plagued with constant bickering, fighting and other dysfunctionalities take their toll, just as divorce headed marriages, except there is no end in sight. But most people don't realize that even those amiable marriages do irreparable harm to those around them and society in general! Let me explain. I'm sure you have all heard the joke about the three golfing (or hunting or fishing) buddies that pause for a moment as a funeral is passing by. The first removes his hat and places it over his heart. The second turns to the third and says "isn't that touching!" to which the third says "Yes, it would have been thirty years today!" The humor here touches on a general feeling that pervades our society today that this is what marriage is really like! It's something you put up with "after the honeymoon is over" because it beats the alternatives as long as it doesn't interfere too much with the more important things in life such as work, sports, leisure or grandkids. This sets our expectations as we grow up and fall in love. We hope that our marriage will be something more, but when it turns out not to be, we conclude that all marriages are like this. It's what we've seen in all the jokes and comic strips, witnessed in our parents, relatives and friend's marriages. That's the way it is; grow up and forget the fairytales, this is real life!

But there are some marriages out there, I'd guess less than 10%, that are different. These are the ones where, despite having been married for a long time, you often see them holding hands. If you pay attention, you'll notice that they <u>never</u> say anything derogatory about their marriage (or marriage in general) or their spouse, whether the spouse is present or not. You may even catch them stealing a kiss or saying "I love you" quietly when they think no one is watching. If you talk to these people about their marriage, you will find that they feel their marriage is the most important thing in their lives. They are more in love now than the day that they got married and it has exceeded all of their "fairytale" expectations for living happily ever after.

Can this be? Can two people really be <u>that</u> happily married in the long run? If a large number of marriages are so disastrous they end up in court and most of the rest fall far short of blissful fairytale expectations, how can this be? If these marriages really exist (and they do!) what does it take? Does it take finding your one in a billion soul mate that is the only person right for you, to make it work? Or can nearly any two compatible people entering into marriage make it to wedded bliss? If so, how? In the following chapters, I will strive to answer these questions.

CHAPTER 2

Love Today

When you were young, do you remember asking your parents or someone older: "How will I know real love when it happens? How will I know it when the right person comes along? What is love or how will it feel?" The answer that you probably got was something like:" I can't explain it to you, but don't worry, when the time comes, you'll know it!" This answer was probably not very satisfying or reassuring, especially considering what was at stake! What if I hold out waiting for this special feeling and it never happens, or worse yet, don't recognize it when it does happen and blow my chance to live "happily ever after"?

Our expectations about love and marriage are based on what we hear and see in our own family, from our friends and what we hear and see in the media. As discussed in the first chapter, unless you were very lucky, what you saw in your own family probably wasn't the ideal that you wanted for your own marriage since most marriages range from disasters ending up in court to mediocre ones in which the people are comfortable living together, but for the most part, are living separate lives. Your family situation was more likely the role model of what you wanted to avoid! Even if you were in the fortunate situation of growing up in a family whose foundation was a great marriage, to use as a role model, you probably still weren't sure you knew the answer to these questions about love and marriage. What you saw glamorized by the media didn't always agree with what you saw in the quiet, stable relationship your parents demonstrated at home.

Your friends didn't necessarily know any more about the answer to these big questions than you did, although some may pretend they did. So, as a result, it usually came down to what you saw in the media (childhood books, movies, television and maybe some romance novels as you grew older) that set your expectations for love and marriage. And what did this media teach us?

LOVE IN THE MEDIA

The word "love" is used in the media in many different ways. I "love" my new car and the way it looks and drives, or I would "love" a cold drink on a hot summer afternoon. These are obviously not related to finding the right marriage partner (I hope!). Another common use (or misuse) of the word "love" is a more acceptable way of referring to sex, such as "let's go upstairs and make love" or for lust as in the old Jim Morrison song "hello, I love you, won't you tell me your name?" While these may be the most common use of the word love in the media, they really don't cause any misunderstanding about marital love because the context is obviously different. While sex is usually a significant part of any good marriage, it's obvious to most people that there needs to be more to a great marriage than sex!

Where the confusion really starts, is when talking about "real love". Most will tell you that there are many kinds of real love. There is the love that a mother has for a child that is different than love between siblings and that is different than the love between two marriage partners. The difference between these various kinds of love will become obvious later, but for now, let's focus on the real love between two people considering entering into marriage.

In this context, I feel the media is fairly consistent. In the previous chapter, I referred to "fairytale" marriages because that is where it all starts in forming our expectations. In nearly every fairytale from the old classics like "Cinderella" or "Sleeping Beauty" to the more current generation's "The Little Mermaid" or "Anastasia", the message is the same: a young man and a young woman have a chance meeting and fall instantly and deeply in love. The remainder of the story narrates how they overcome the cruel or evil forces that are keeping them apart. Eventually, good wins out over evil, and the two are reunited and live happily ever after. As you get older, the form of the media changes but the storyline doesn't! Many women like to read romance novels. Think of your favorite ones. In nearly every case, a man has a chance meeting with some woman and they quickly fall deeply in love, but some set of circumstances prevent them from getting together. The situation is usually compounded by poor communications between the couple; some misunderstanding or innocent deceit that gets out of hand. Eventually the truth comes out or the misunderstanding is rectified, and the evil is stopped, allowing them to get back together and live happily ever after. On occasion, since this is an adult media, the evil may win, preventing them from getting back together and you have a classic "tragedy" as in "Romeo and Juliet" or "West Side Story". Whether it's a romance novel, play or movie, they follow the same line: boy and girl meet, fall in love, are forced apart by some circumstance and the remainder of the story is how they get back together, sometimes successfully, sometimes not.

So what do we learn from all of this? Since the media is our main and most prevalent source of input on romance, what expectations does it leave us with? That love is mysterious; you don't know when it will happen to you, or with whom, but you'll know it when it happens! This sounds suspiciously like what your parents told you when you were a kid asking "How will I know?"

Hopefully, many of you reading this have already had some firsthand experience with falling in love. It's a great feeling that I wish everyone would have a chance to experience at some time. Some describe it as a euphoric feeling, like floating with your feet a few inches off the ground. Of course, this other person is a great person. They are not only attractive, but have a great smile that warms you through and through and their sense of humor keeps you laughing all the time. They are smart, generous and thoughtful and so easy to be around. This other person seems to know your thoughts and, therefore, must be your soul mate. They are completely trustworthy and dependable and, on the rare occasion that they were not, there were extenuating circumstances that forced them to be that way; some of which was probably your fault. Everything is right with the world! You want to be with the object of your affection constantly, nothing else seems to matter. Being apart from them is actually painful. You are only fully happy when you are around them and don't care what other people think if they are critical. This feeling of love is definitely what you want to feel for the rest of your life, and this is the person you want to feel it with!

CHAPTER 3

So what is the problem?

OK, so now it has finally happened! You've met that special someone and have fallen deeply in love. It feels just like the fairytales, romance novels and movies said it would! You didn't plan it, but it just happened and it's real and you know it just like your parents said! You feel great and for the first time, you feel complete around this other person. You may get some static from your parents or your friends, but they are just being overly protective or maybe in some cases, a little jealous, but they don't know this other person like you do. After all, there are always obstacles in life, but love conquers all eventually! This feeling of love continuesto grow stronger month after month and you are sure that you want to spend the rest of your life with this person. You are sure that it would make no difference if they were richer or poorer, in good health or bad; you want to "have them and hold them until death do you part". So you arrange for the wedding ceremony and finally take the solemn vow to love them for the rest of your life!!

<u>**Now think about this!**</u> You are vowing for the rest of your life to have a feeling for another person? A feeling that you had no control over its onset in the first place? If you had no choice about "falling into it" in the first place, what makes you think you won't "fall out of it", with no choice, in the future? **You can't rationallypromise something you have no control over!!**

Science has come to understand that this euphoric feeling that most people (with the help of the media) associate with "falling in love" is the release of a strong chemical in your brain called "dopamine". This chemical operates in the pleasure centers of your brain, like other narcotics, and is a natural reward system for doing the right things to continue your blood line (in this case, identifying a potential mate). This chemical is so strong, it often leads to behaviors that you might otherwise think are irrational. To get a feel for how strong dopamine is, consider some of the actions that adolescents do to attract members of the opposite sex after reaching puberty compared with pre-pubescence when even the thought of hanging around with the opposite sex was "yucky". The way they dress, wear their hair, adorn themselves with jewelry, drinking, smoking, defying authority, showing off, being part of the "desirable" group or being independent can all be instinctive ways of showing that you are good mating material! And if you have "fallen in love", even very recently, and a conflict develops between your lifelong best friend and this potential mate, the friend will lose every time until the dopamine wanes. Until you actually witness this happen in someone you know well, you can't believe it is that strong!

The really dangerous part of dopamine is that it will distort your view of the object of your affection. All positive attributes will be enhanced: the person will seem more physically attractive than others see them, smarter, kinder, more generous, and of course have a great sense of humor. Even worse, dopamine will mask negative qualities. This is why people who "fall in love" often don't seem to recognize the obvious faults of the person they love. Other friends will ask each other, "What do they see in them?" If a well intentioned friend or relative tries to point out some negative characteristic, or lack of a positive characteristic, the person in love will reject the facts saying that he or she is "not really that way, you just don't know them or understand".

Unfortunately, this dopamine high can last for a long time, even stretching into years. When finally the production of dopamine wanes, the person "falls out of love" and wonders what they ever saw in this jerk in the first place, or more likely concludes that the person has "changed". The fact of the matter is that most people cannot and do

14

not change their personalities as an adult. Scientists, through the study of identical twins, are finding that a lot of our personality is genetically based; we are born with them and cannot change them. Some small portion of our basic personality can be environmentally induced, but this usually happens before age four. Behaviors, on the other hand, result from a combination of your personality and environmental learning and can change. As an adult, however, it requires a great deal of effort. So if this sensitive, thoughtful, caring and otherwise neat person you fell in love with, turns out to be an insensitive, cruel, self centered slob, chances are, you were suffering from dopamine distortion as opposed to them really having changed. Unfortunately, by the time the dopamine wanes, it's too late. You are already married and perhaps raising a family.

I remember one seminar I attended, that cautioned it was risky to get married in the first two years after meeting someone because you may have a very distorted view of them due to dopamine. Since waiting that long is often not reasonable to many, there are a couple of telltale signs that you should be aware of that are clues that your view may be distorted. One such clue is if you don't like the people your fiancé hangs around with. The old adage that "birds of a feather flock together" is generally true. It would be unusual for people with different value systems and life philosophies to be close friends. Therefore, if you don't like your fiancés' friends, you are probably not getting an accurate view of your fiancé. Another clue is if your own best friends, the people you like, trust and share a lot with, don't like your fiancé or at least wonder what you see in him or her; it is likely that they are seeing more clearly than you because they are <u>not</u> suffering from dopamine distortion of this person. Unfortunately, they must tread very carefully here because the dopamine will drive you to reject the truth and end the friendship rather than recognize the problem with your potential mate!

If you ask a young person who is considering marriage, what "love" is, there will typically be a long pause followed by "It's hard to explain". As a technical person, I find it very unsettling that marriage, the most important contract in most people's lives, is usually based on a promise of something that they admit they don't really understand. "It's a mystery, but you'll know it when it comes along!" What other kind of important contract would people enter into, knowing fully they don't understand it? Yet most people seem to accept this confusion: "it's love; it's a feeling, it's romantic, it's not something that you can pin down and understand!"

Our expectation, based on all we have been taught, is that once we find this love, we will live happily ever after. So we make the vow to "love", without understanding that it is mostly a trick our bodies are playing on us and is destined to wane at some point in the future, usually in the first few years of a marriage when "the honeymoon is over". Is it any wonder then that a large number of marriages in our country run into trouble and many of them in the first three to five years? What they are based on has gone away! When this happens, all that is left may be the hassles: "I never get out and have fun anymore!", "I never have enough money!", "All I do is clean up after the kids!", "I don't get to see my friends!", "Life is boring!", "All we do is bicker and fight!", "What was I thinking?", "Marriage is a pain in the . . ."

Unfortunately, once the dopamine wanes with your spouse, it can start all over again with any acquaintance at work or in the neighborhood, that your subconscious thinks is another potential mate. The same kind of distortions to rational thought can trick you into thinking "it's okay to flirt, I'm just having a little fun, I won't let it go too far!", or later on "no one will notice, we won't get caught". It will also distort your view of the new object of your affection such as "he really loves me and will eventually leave his wife" despite all evidence to the contrary. Or, "this is really the perfect person for me, my soul mate; it was destined to be!" And the carnage in relationships continues!

Don't get me wrong! The euphoric feeling of love, caused by dopamine, is a great thing and probably even necessary. In fact, if you don't feel it for the person you want to marry, there may be something wrong! But it's what we call in mathematics a "necessary but not sufficient condition". In other words, you need to feel this way about the person you want to marry, but it is not enough to base the marriage on!

CHAPTER 4

Love

About ten years into my own marriage, I happened to pick up the book "*The Road Less Traveled*" by Dr. M. Scott Peck. In the early chapters, Dr. Peck explains that the problems most people have in life are actually caused by themselves trying to avoid something uncomfortable. Let me give you a simple example from my own life. As a child, I didn't like the taste of most vegetables. Canned peas or corn were okay but carrots or canned spinach was terrible! My parents, however, expected and insisted that I eat what was given to me. The meat and potatoes were great and I would eat them right down, but the pile of spinach was dreaded and avoided. I'd push it around with my fork and spread it out so that it might look like I ate some, but my parents were seldom fooled, so they would eventually tell me that I had to eat most of what was there on my plate or go to my room for the evening. (This was before the days of computers, electronic games and cell phones that make staying in your room desirable!) By this time the spinach was stone cold, but I'd put some in my mouth and gag and cry. My parents would then send me to my room where I would spend the rest of the evening with the terrible taste of cold canned spinach in my mouth. Dr. Peck's philosophy says that what I should have done, is to recognize that I had to eat the spinach, so go ahead and get it over with while it was still warm and a least somewhat palatable. Then I could eat the rest of my meal happy, knowing that the bad part was behind me! I would have ended the meal with a good taste in my mouth and have the rest of the evening to go and play with my friends!

You can apply this same philosophy to all aspects of your life: recognize that there will be things in your life that will be unfair and unpleasant. When they show up, rather than trying to find ways to avoid them (such as procrastinating, lying, or cheating), just step up, admit they exist and get them behind you as soon as possible. In doing so, life ahead of you becomes easier. (This is the path <u>less</u> traveled.) Instead most people try to avoid the discomfort by lying or finding a short cut (the path <u>more</u> traveled); however, typically the problem only gets worse and more complicated as the tangled web of avoidance lies grows, and the basic problem is still there.

Dr. Peck's philosophy made a great deal of sense to me so I was interested in reading on. Soon I got to the part where he defined "love". His definition was: "a conscious decision to do whatever was required to nurture the spiritual growth of another". **WHAT???** I immediately rejected this definition thinking "has this poor man never experienced that great feeling of real love?" I was happily married and this great feeling had always been a big part of it. I put the book down thinking this man was obviously wrong and therefore, there was no sense reading further as I could no longer trust it to be correct.

At about this same time, our marriage was having a problem, but I was unaware of it. We had gotten married just as we were finishing our undergraduate education and I took an engineering job in the mid-west, 500 miles from where we both had been born and raised in upstate New York. My wife's degree was in nursing which allowed her to be able to find a job anywhere she wanted. This relocation had effectively cut us both off from our families and previous friends, but that was no big problem. We had each other and that was all we needed. My concept of marriage at that time was very much along the line "and the two shall become one". Our jobs kept us apart while at work; but, I felt that all of our spare time and recreation should be spent together. Since I had the more aggressive personality and liked physical outdoor activity, our recreational activities centered around hiking, biking, skiing, snowmobiles, dirt bikes, cars, etc. My wife, having grown up in a household with a <u>very</u> dominating father, was very good at appeasement and peace-keeping and went along with my notions, and even enjoyed most of them. All of our friends were either couples from the neighborhood, or couples that I had met the husband at work. I considered us very happily married!

One day, my wife approached me and told me that she was starting to feel suffocated in our relationship of always doing everything together and always what I wanted. She said she felt she needed to develop friends and hobbies that didn't necessarily include me. I was shocked and devastated! Wasn't this what marriage was all about: two becoming one? I felt our doing everything together was a sign of how strong our love was. Did this mean her love for me was waning? Had she met someone else? Was this the beginning of the end? I took a number of long walks to try to figure out where we had gone wrong.

As we talked it out, she assured me that none of my fears were true, she just needed room to grow. I realized that giving up control was against my nature, but I had no choice. If she was unhappy, our marriage was doomed anyway, so it was worth the try. I feared she would want separate vacations and would eventually meet other men and all was lost, but, in reality, all she wanted was my understanding that if she wanted to go away for a weekend with girl friends at work, or take up a new hobby that I wasn't interested in, or spend some evenings at night school learning new skills, it was okay.

As the months went by, she started cultivating a few new friends from work and took up some new hobbies and seemed happier. Nothing bad came of it and my fears gradually eased. In fact, I started to realize that our marriage was even better than before because she was happier.

A couple of years later, I picked up Dr. Peck's book and started reading it all over again. When I got to the part about his definition of love, that I had previously rejected, it suddenly dawned on me what had happened! In our marriage, I had been willing to do what was necessary for her growth and our marriage had grown! Was this purely coincidental? Was I the one who was wrong and he was right? Was Dr.

Peck's definition of love a new concept? Is there some way to verify that it is valid and really works? These questions flooded my mind and I set out to find the answers. It was an epiphany!

The first step was to figure out how his definition was really different from my own previous concept. The *American Heritage College Dictionary* defines love as "a deep, tender feeling of affection and solicitude toward a person . . ." The main focus of love by this definition (and the use in previous chapters) is the self; it is something you feel, you need, you want. The focus of this love is what it does to or for you. In Dr. Peck's definition, however, the focus is the "other" with no regard, in fact, for how it makes you feel or what you need or what you want. This is a **HUGE** difference! Is real love a "self centered" feeling as the dictionary says and the media portrays or is it an "other centered" action as Dr. Peck promotes? As a first test, for example, consider your marriage vows. How can you vow to feel a certain way for the rest of your life? It doesn't make sense! You can, however, vow to dedicate your actions toward the growth of another person for the rest of your life. It does make sense, but is it really what love is all about?

In the marriage preparation programs that I previously alluded to, one minor aspect of the program is to help the couple plan the wedding ceremony including which scripture readings they would like to use. One of the most popular ones was from the New Testament of the Bible: 1 Corinthians 13, in which Paul describes love. Paul writes "love" is never jealous, never rude, never thinks evil of another, never seeks to promote itself and never lies. Instead, it will bear all things without concern for itself, seeks only truth and never fails. Now let's compare how the two definitions of love stand up to this description. The self centered feeling definition of love in the dictionary and other media, often leads to jealousy and is easily hurt and all the rest of the things the Bible says it should not be (but it makes for a good story line). Dr. Peck's definition, on the other hand, fits perfectly! If your focus is only on helping the other person grow, certainly you would not be jealous of their interactions with others, you would not be rude to them or think evil of them, and never lie to them; you are trying to help them. Instead, you would always hope for the best for them, seek the truth for them, work for their growth and be willing to bear discomfort for the other, if that's what it takes. This is in perfect agreement with Paul's description!

While trying to figure out a way to verify if Dr. Peck's definition is really a valid definition of love, it appears that I may have stumbled across, perhaps, the most authoritative validation of all times: the Bible. That also answers the question of whether Dr. Peck's definition represents new and original thinking; it is an excellent description of the life of Christ. He devoted his life to loving others, always focusing on how to help the other person grow spiritually to be the best they can be, as in Dr. Peck's definition. And he told us to do likewise!

REAL MARITAL LOVE

There are two very different definitions of love that may be on a person's mind as they recite their marriage vows:

1. The feeling that started when they "fell in love" with the other person and was promoted in media since childhood. Unfortunately, this feeling is not something you can vow because you have no control over it, it will eventually wane and when it does, if that is what your marriage was based on, the result will be disillusionment at best or divorce at worst.

2. The "other centered" definition offered by Dr. Peck. This is the only one that makes sense to vow to another person for the rest of your life and in fact, has been the recommended approach since "biblical times".

In actuality, you should have both. While the "other centered" love is what you can and should mean in your vows, if you don't <u>feel</u> the strong physical and emotional attraction for the other person, there may be something very wrong going on. I've had people tell me that although they didn't feel that strong physical attraction for the other person, they went ahead and got married anyway and expected that it would come later. Unfortunately, for them, that's not how it usually works. The fantastic feeling of falling in love can happen "at first sight", or over the course of hours, weeks or months; whatever it takes for your subconscious to recognize that the other person is a potential mate and start pumping out the dopamine to make sure it happens. But if it doesn't happen by the time you have decided to marry, it probably won't. So if you don't feel it, you need to figure out why before making a life commitment. In one case I am familiar with, the person later realized that the marriage was actually just a means of escape from an undesirable home situation rather than any kind of love for the other person. In another, the person realized they were homosexual. Whatever the reason, figure it out before you make the leap!

In most cases however, the feeling comes first and it is strong. It's a great feeling that I hope everyone feels at some point, enjoy the ride! But be warned: it is not sufficient to base a marriage on because it will diminish or go away completely at some point in time.

The "other center" love, being a conscious decision to devote your life to helping this other person, can happen whenever you choose. Ideally, it comes before the wedding and is the basis of your vows. In most cases however, it comes well into the marriage, if at all. Better late than never! The risk is that after the dopamine wanes, negative events take place that will prevent you from ever wanting to make the other centered commitment.

CHAPTER 5

So Why Doesn't Everyone?

I f this other centered understanding of marital love has been around for so long and is so effective, why isn't it the norm? After all, things that work well, usually get noticed and copied. I believe there are many reasons that other centered is not the norm and they include the following:

1.) There is the basic misunderstanding of love that has just been discussed: we are bombarded day in and day out with the wrong description. Pick any form of popular media and conduct your own survey; be it television, music, movies or any other. Look for the use of the word love pertaining to the relationship between two adults. Keep track as to whether the context was "self centered" (I feel, I want, or I need) or "other centered" (for the benefit of another, even at the expense of self). My little surveys show "other centered" less than 10% of the time. How are people, especially inexperienced people with hormones raging, supposed to pick out the proper understanding when the wrong understanding is the vast majority of what they are bombarded with? Is the media simply the reflection of our times or the cause of it? That is a debate that goes well beyond the scope of this book, but few will disagree that the message is very lopsided toward self centered unless you spend a lot of time watching "Touched by an Angel" reruns. The result is most people enter into marriage with the mindset of how good this feels to me and, therefore, how good it will feel in the future. Unfortunately, when the future arrives and the dopamine driven good feelings wane, and the hassles of life dominate your day, the media is right there to reinforce that it's okay; everybody feels that way. From the "Lockhorns" comic strip, the negative comments that you hear from your friends at work about their spouse, to the continual stream of stories in the news about celebrities and politicians acting badly; that's just the way it is! Your earlier delusions of living "happily ever after" must never have been realistic in the first place. You may even conclude that these fantastic "live happily ever after" marriages don't really exist at all or are just mis-rememberances of some old people trying to justify why they stuck it out together for fifty years! The shame of it all is that these marriages <u>do</u> exist, and in fact, are within the grasp of nearly everyone if they want it!

2.) Another reason "other centered" is not the norm is that the benefits are not as obvious in this self centered world. The rewards of immediate gratification are quite obvious; everything else is a little bit vague. However, what if you were told that the benefits of "other centered" marital love continue to grow over time and bring good feelings and happiness that are even <u>better</u> than the feeling of falling in love the first time! And, unlike the dopamine driven feelings, will continue to grow ever stronger over time, rather than wane. Starting in the next chapter, we'll start to explore the benefits of "other centered" love and I hope to convince you that the benefits <u>far</u> outweigh self centered love.

3.) As mentioned earlier, Paul's description of love in the Bible says that it never promotes itself. This works against its spread! The couples that have this kind of love, don't go around bragging about it; that's a putdown of the majority and it's obvious to them most people wouldn't believe it anyway! The only evidence that these marriages exist at all is when you notice this couple seems to have something different and better in their marriage than most. If you are not looking for it because you assume such marriages don't exist, it's easy to overlook the signs.

4.) Finally, behaving in an "other centered" way is often seen as not easy. This is true, at least at first. First it requires that you must try to understand what the other person's needs are. This is not easy because needs and wants are often very different things. An alcoholic may tell you he/she needs another drink when the opposite is actually true. It takes time and communication and work to be able to fulfill your vow of love; to really help the other person. It's like the old adage "give a person a fish and you will relieve their hunger for a day; teach the person to fish and you will relieve their hunger for a lifetime!" Luckily, the more you do it, the more you really understand the other and the easier it becomes to figure out their real needs. Perhaps even more difficult is assessing your own actions for their <u>real</u> motivation. It's easy to say your spouse doesn't need something, when in reality, it's just an excuse to avoid some cost or inconvenience to yourself. Likewise, it's easy to say your spouse needs something, when in reality, it's something you want. An open and honest appraisal of your own motives is frequently uncomfortable and only comes with dedication and maturity. You will find that your partner will often have better insight into your motives than you do, at first, if you are willing to take this assessment constructively rather than as an affront. As with most things, practice makes perfect and the more you do it, the easier it gets.

With all of these factors going against it, it's no wonder "other centered" marriages are not the norm. Unfortunately, it results in most people missing out on the greatest opportunity of their life!

CHAPTER 6

Growth

So why would I want to get involved in this other centered love? Why would I want to devote my life to helping <u>another</u> person to become the best that <u>they</u> can be? It doesn't sound like fun; I'm not Mother Theresa and don't want to be!

One reason is our own personal growth. Don't laugh! Think back to your own experience where you have grown as a person. Maybe it's when you have achieved something that you have been working hard for, such as a college degree, or have mastered some new skill, such as playing a musical instrument. Maybe it's when some experience has given you a new perspective of something, perhaps overcoming a prejudice that you now realize was untrue. Often, growth comes after a difficult time or a situation that forces you to change, and gives you a new perspective of things in the aftermath. For some, it may be a religious experience. Doesn't it make you feel good that you have grown? Would you ever want to go back to your less mature self, even though it may have seemed easier (ignorance is bliss)? Some may call it emotional growth or spiritual growth, but it's the maturing of our understanding of reality and ourselves and then acting consistently with that understanding to become the best person we can be. I'll call it personal growth.

I believe we all have an innate desire for personal growth. We all think that we have learned a lot and are fairly mature in our world views. While many people do continue to learn and grow to become better people throughout their lives, the pace usually slows for most people as we get set in our ways and see less need to change. In other words, become too comfortable with where or who we are. In the worst case, some people get stuck at some level of maturity and will not grow without some help to get them "unstuck". I suspect most people in this situation don't realize that they need help until a traumatic experience such as job loss or a divorce makes it difficult to avoid the fact that something is wrong and needs to change. Even then, the other person or the world is first suspected to be the problem.

Regardless of your situation, personal growth is seldom easy. It usually means putting aside some belief you have about yourself or others or relationships that is not true or accurate and replacing it with a belief that is more true or more accurate. Admitting that something that you have believed all your life is not true is hard enough for most people, but adding on the fear of the unknown that is associated with significant change, results in pretty slow progress for most of us if we try to go it alone.

It should be obvious, however, that regardless of where you are on the personal growth scale, or how fast you are or are not moving, getting the right assistance can speed the progress up and get you closer to your goal of becoming the best you can be. Some small number of people get professional assistance, however, most don't because of some of the negatives associated with that. It's usually expensive, there is a lingering stigma that psychiatrists only treat "crazy" people and it's hard to find a good one (as with any profession, there is a vast range of capabilities out there)! And finally, it is by nature a slow process because even the best psychiatrist needs to get to know and understand you before they can help you; and at an hour a week, that can take years. Most people, therefore, go it alone, some actively seeking opportunities for growth, others only doing so by accident if at all.

Now consider this: what if you had a person with you every day whose main goal in life was to help you grow? Additionally, this person knows you better than you probably do yourself and you trust that this person will always do and say whatever is needed to help you become a better person. This person can be counted on to say only the truth and you have learned from experience that this is always the case. You don't always like what you hear, but you have confidence that what the other is saying they believe to be the truth and are saying it only to help you, not punish you. Furthermore, you can tell this person anything you think or feel with full confidence that it will never be used against you and will never be told to another living soul, if you want it that way. If this were the case, wouldn't your rate of personal growth improve dramatically? It would be like having your own personal psychiatrist with you to ask questions of and help you as you go through life! In the other centered definition of marital love, this is <u>exactly</u> what your spouse has vowed to do. Furthermore, you have vowed to return the same assistance!

This mutual assistance vow carries with it a large responsibility. If you are going to help each other in this very important way, you must develop the trust between you that the other person really has <u>your</u> best interests at heart. If you are going to have to change your perceptions in order to grow, you <u>must</u> be able to trust that what the other person is telling you is true and not just a manipulation for selfish reasons on their part. Likewise, you have to be continually questioning your own motives in the relationship to make sure you really do have the best interests of the other person at heart, not just trying to change them to make your own life easier. You have to be scrupulously honest about it with yourself. But if both parties try to keep that vow, and when pointed out that they are not acting accordingly, try to do better rather than become defensive; eventually the trust grows, the assistance is taken and both people start growing much faster than they ever could on their own!

I have personally benefited tremendously in this respect. There have been many more times than I would like to admit that my wife has come to me at the appropriate time and said "you should call your brother and see how he is doing", or "I think you may have hurt this person's feelings, you should call and make amends", or "what can we do to help this person that is in need" or even, "I think you are starting to drink too much on weekends". I don't always like to hear these words but I know she is right and has my best interests at heart. Most of what I have learned on how to truly love, I've learned from her coaching and example and am a far better person for it.

There will be set backs; we are only human and therefore, will make mistakes. The important thing is that when mistakes happen and both parties recognize that it was a mistake, you go back to the concept of other centered love, that you have vowed, and try your best to get it right. The most difficult of these possible mistakes is when one partner has been unfaithful (engaged in extramarital sex). This is particularly devastating because, unlike something said in anger at the spur of the moment and then regretted, it's typically something that came about over the course of weeks, months or even years. And during this time, the perpetrator was not only interested in just themselves, but had full knowledge that (because of the intimacy of their betrayal) their actions would cause great pain to the person they had vowed to help. The ability to trust that the other person will, in the future, have your best interests at heart, rather than their own, has been destroyed and will take a long time and a lot of work just to get back to the starting point of your marriage, let alone make significant progress. In my work with couples engaged to be married, I would ask them what would happen if they were ever to find out that their partner had been unfaithful. The answer was nearly always, without hesitation, that it would end their marriage! I would then immediately recommend that they consider modifying the wedding vows that they were going to recite to read ". . . until death or unfaithfulness do us part." The dead silence that would follow would only be broken by them saying "I get your point!" The fact of the matter is, the other centered love that you have vowed demands that you forgive and help your spouse overcome this weakness and become a better person, regardless of the pain that it has brought to you.

It's like two people climbing a rugged mountain; two people with a rope connecting them can climb higher, faster and safer than either can do on their own. The climbing team can help each other get across barriers that they could not do themselves. And when one person makes a mistake, that's when the rope is really needed! As in marriage, that is not the time to cut the rope because the other person made a mistake. Use the rope with patience and forgiveness to help the other person figure out what went wrong so that it can be avoided next time. The team will be stronger, better climbers as a result. And besides, the next time, it may be you who makes the mistake and you need that same response!

So, if you and your partner view your marriage as the other centered kind, as discussed above, you can expect personal growth far beyond anything you could ever achieve yourself!

Now, if that were as far as it goes, it seems this promise of personal growth should be enough to motivate most people to want to do it, since we all want to grow. But that is not even the half of it: the best benefits are to come! Read on!

CHAPTER 7

Happiness

At this point, some people may be thinking "Yeah, yeah, this is all well and good, I'm all for personal growth, but this dedicating my life to what is good for another person doesn't sound like a lot of fun! I want to enjoy my life, too!" Or as Billy Joel's song "Virginia" says, "I'd rather laugh with the sinners than cry with the saints".

Let's take a closer look at happiness. What is it that makes people happy? I feel happy when I get a new car or anything material that I have wanted for some time. People often think "if I only had more money, I would be happier because I could get anything I wanted". But if money or material things were really a source of true happiness, then rich people would all be happy people and poor people would be sad people. Daily news about celebrities quickly dispels that notion; in fact, some might argue that even the opposite may be true! In my experience, the happiness of acquiring some new thing quickly wears off with time, and the more you acquire, the less important each new thing is to you.

The same logic holds true for fame or power. If these were real sources of happiness, then famous or powerful people would be happier people than the rest of us, and again, this is obviously not the case!

So what is a real and long term source of happiness? How about a source of happiness that not only made you happy when it happened, but makes you just as happy when you remember it twenty years later? In addition, the more it happens, the <u>greater</u> the resulting happiness is, each time? That would be a real source of happiness!

Have you ever been in the situation where someone really needed help and you were the only person who could or would help them, and you did so without any consideration of being paid back or even recognized for your good deed? Perhaps it was a scared child separated from its parents in a large store, or an elderly person stranded with car troubles and no phone, or giving food, clothing or shelter to a person who just lost everything in a fire or other disaster, or maybe just giving a listening ear to a friend that is struggling with life or even death.

When I have helped people in this way, it made me feel good at the time, makes me happy when I remember it, and would make me feel even better if the opportunity came along more often! This fits the bill of a true source of happiness! In addition, the more important the help rendered, the greater the happiness derived; holding a door for a person is good, but saving their life is even better. The problem with getting happiness in this way is that opportunities to <u>really</u> help people don't usually come along all that often. How many times in the past year have you come across a stranded person or lost child? Opportunities to help a person emotionally or spiritually may be one of the most important ways you can help someone, but the opportunities are even more limited because you need to really understand the person or the situation well enough to know what is going on before you can effectively help.

Now, look at the other centered marriage situation. In this case, you are helping the other person with perhaps the most important thing in their life; their personal growth. You are the only person in the world with the proper knowledge of them and the earned trust to be able to help them. Suppose you were able to help this other person overcome an addiction that was killing them. Suppose you were responsible for convincing another person to continue on or go back to school that allowed the person to blossom in an area that they were meant to excel in. Suppose you were responsible for a person's religious conversion that turns their life around. Suppose you were instrumental in helping another person recognize where pride, competitiveness or misconceptions had soured their relationship with friends or siblings or parents or even their own children. Imagine the feeling of seeing them embrace with love, a relationship that had previously only brought pain, all because of your intervention. The happiness that you will feel by watching this other person grow in response to your help and trust will over shadow any happiness brought by material things or self centered actions and it can happen every day, not just once in a while!

This is not to say that you should not indulge in the other more short term or self centered sources of happiness; the new car, the golf clubs or the cold beer when working on a hot afternoon. Enjoy them all! The only restriction is that they cannot be in conflict with your promise to help the other. The car can't be instead of the college education your partner needs or the cold beer can't be fueling an addiction that is hurting you and the people around you.

So if you think that a marriage based on other centered love would deprive you of some fun and happiness, just the opposite is true; you can still have all the fun you want, but it offers a level of happiness that self centered pursuits never can.

But that's not all, it gets even better!

CHAPTER 8

The Spiral

You saw in previous chapters that if you realize that love is the other centered commitment to help another grow, marriage based on this understanding, is an unparalleled opportunity for two people to experience personal growth because of the unique knowledge they have of each other and the amount of time they can spend together. Growing in this way makes you a better person and makes you feel very good about yourself. In the last chapter, you saw that helping your spouse in this very important way will bring you great happiness and not just on the rare occasion, but nearly every day. Human nature is such that things that make you happy, especially those that make you feel good about yourself, tend to want to be repeated often. The more you do it, the more comfortable you become with it and the better you get at it. This in turn, results in more growth and more happiness and the desire for more! **A couple gets caught up in this upward spiral of loving, helping, growing and happiness that has no upward limit; it just keeps getting better! The marriage becomes the focal point for your fulfillment and happiness. You have become one of those rare cases mentioned in Chapter 1 in which the marriage has become the most important thing in your life because it is the source of all happiness and growth. And you are more in love now than the day you got married, by far.**

CHAPTER 9

Honesty and Respect

By now you should realize that this spiral of love, growth and happiness is based completely on trust; trust that what the other person is telling you is both true and selfless if you are to benefit from it. This will take time and continual effort to demonstrate to the other that this is the case. Trust that the other person is always telling the truth is a fragile thing. A single incident of not being truthful can wipe out years of trust building and the lie does not have to be a big one. When we catch a person even in a small lie, we immediately conclude that if this person is not truthful in this small thing, why should I believe that they are completely truthful when the stakes are high?

Some time back, my wife and I were with a woman that I liked and respected. We asked if she would like to join us for dinner. She replied that her husband was expecting her home soon, but she would just tell him that she had to work late. I was astounded that she would lie about something so unimportant! If she would lie about this, she certainly would lie about anything, if she "had" to. Although, as a couple, they seemed happy and doing well at the time, I was not surprised when a few years later, they were "suddenly" divorced. There is no one that is so skilled at lying that they won't get caught in it at some time, because you never know what other people may know from other sources. And once caught, the trust will be very hard to come by that they will not lie in the future. So if you are a person that thinks "little white lies" are okay, this type of marital bliss I've been describing will never happen.

I also don't think that it is possible to be completely truthful to one person, but not all others. If your spouse sees you lying to other people when convenient, they will never have the trust that you won't lie to them when the truth is difficult. **So with this lifelong vow to love another, must come a lifelong vow of absolutetruth to all. You can't have one without the other!**

Some people will say "I have to lie sometimes to keep from hurting another person's feelings!" I think this is the proverbial "slippery slope". If you have to make value judgments of a situation to determine whether or not to lie, I'm not confident that high levels of dopamine in some situations can't sway those judgments to the wrong conclusion. Certainly, truth should never be used for the sole purpose of hurting someone's feelings and withholding truth can be considered lying in many situations. When faced with this situation, it's usually best to just shut your mouth and walk away. At least that way, you've spared someone's feelings and can still feel good about never having told a lie when the truth will do no good.

Another thing that should be obvious by now is that for this spiral to work, there must be great mutual respect. If you are to be willing to devote the rest of your life to them, you must have great respect for them. And that means respect for them as they are now, not someone you think they can become in the future with your help. If there is something about them that you don't respect, beware! Are you willing to accept this trait, as is, for the rest of your life? People's personalities usually don't change; much of who we are is genetically set at birth and is difficult to hide, let alone change. Aspects that you don't respect about a person, may not be changeable, even if they successfully grow to be a better person. **So if you don't respect them as anequal, are you really willing to put them first for therest of your life? Probably not!**

The respect must be mutual! If you detect any sign ofabuse from your mate, emotional or physical, they donot respect you and it will not work; get out! Physical abuse is fairly easy to recognize; purposeful infliction of pain to motivate or punish should never be tolerated in a relationship. Emotional abuse is harder to recognize because it requires assessing the motivation. If you feel hurt by something that was said, are they really trying to help you see how to become a better person or are they punishing you for some self centered need? One is love, the other is abuse. Even lectures or scoldings can be a sign that they don't respect you as an equal and are therefore, not ready for other centered love; they are still centered on self. **If your partner doesn't respect you as an equal, it's unlikely they will dedicate their life to helping you.**

The other requirement of respect is that it must be based on truly knowing who the other person is, and this takes time. It takes seeing the other person in all types of situations and going through all types of feelings, and then deeply communicating about it with you to really get a sense of who they are. This can't happen in a week or a month. **Until you have spent the time to really know each other, you can't know if you respect each other enough to dedicate the rest of your life to putting them first.**

But if you really know and respect each other now, that will only grow as you grow.

CHAPTER 10

Other Connections

At this point, I'd like to point out a couple of other aspects of other-centered love that do not directly relate to the marriage situation:

REACHING OUT

Another benefit of other-centered love, as you learn and practice it with your spouse, is that it makes it easier and more comfortable to reach out to others around you; your family, your friends, neighbors and the people you work with day in and day out. Fairly frequently in your life, you probably come across relatives, friends or co-workers that could use a little emotional or spiritual help. Signs could be the person being in a bad mood or getting angry at things that normally wouldn't bother them or perhaps being unusually withdrawn or distracted. The strongest sign is if it appears that the person may have been crying when no one was around. You may feel that you would like to help them but don't know how. A few previous experiences in your life on "butting in" on this kind of thing may not have been very successful so you are too uncomfortable or embarrassed to risk saying anything. It's easier to say to yourself, "It's not my business, if they want help, they will ask for it." But, in fact, they are no better at communicating on these types of subjects than you are. They have no reason to believe

38

that you could or would help them and therefore are too embarrassed to ask. As a result, an opportunity to help another human being is missed. If, however, for years, you have had this mindset that when you see that your spouse is troubled, you need to stop what you are doing and step in, you actually have a great deal of experience in these matters. You have found that at times there is nothing wrong, or at least nothing that they care to share at this point in time. More frequently, all that is needed is a listening ear of someone who won't judge or gossip, and having noticed that you always seem honest and truthful, may be willing to open up to you confidentially. They don't really want your advice on how to solve their problems, they just need to get it "off their chest" and in the process of explaining it to you, not only feel better, but may gain some insight or perspective that actually helps them. You may even have found that on rare occasions, you have the experience, knowledge or connections that can actually help them solve their problem. Armed with the confidence this experience brings, you are much more likely to offer help. This not only helps them but helps you to become a better and more understanding person, which, in turn, brings more happiness and growth to you and the people around you.

If on occasion, a person actually seeks your advice on how to solve a personal problem, be very cautious as your ability to help is limited by your understanding of the person and the situation and things are often not what they seem. It takes a great deal of listening and thought before you can really understand. Once again, your spouse, because of your mutual trust and experience in loving, can offer a great sounding board, perspective and insight that you may otherwise miss. My wife, for instance, has much better intuitive instincts about people, even if having met them only briefly. I have learned to trust her intuition which has allowed me to defuse problems at work before they get out of hand. Likewise, my strong points have always been in thinking and planning logically. I can help her as she attempts to help others, allowing her to get to the real root cause so that it can be fixed or avoided in the future. **Because of our love and trust of each other, we are better at loving others.**

<u>LOVE REVISITED</u>

Earlier in this book, while discussing "real love", I mentioned the commonly held belief that real love between a man and a woman was different than that of a mother for her child or between siblings. It should be obvious by now, that the definition of other-centered love (a conscious decision to help another person grow) works well for all of these! In addition, Christians are called to "love" their neighbor. Certainly, Christ was not asking people to have a euphoric feeling for their neighbor; he was telling them to help each other selflessly. Any scientist will tell you that the simpler and universally applicable a principle is, the more likely it is true. If a principle requires different versions for different applications, it has probably missed the point. For me, this goes a long way in proving the dictionary is wrong and Dr. Peck is right when it comes to love.

CHAPTER 11

Q & A

I believe that for most people in this country, the subject of love and marriage is either a big mystery or is misunderstood, and this lack of understanding ultimately leads to the high divorce rate we see today. This is true whether you are an adolescent contemplating it for the first time, a young adult who has "fallen in love" (or would like to) and is wondering what the future holds, or a married person who has found that "living happily ever after" didn't come true.

The mystery, depending on your stage of life, revolves around one or both of the following questions:

- Who is the right person for me and how will I know?

- Can I really expect to live "happily ever after"?

In the introduction to this book, I made the seemingly outrageous claim that there is a single simple principle, that once understood and followed, <u>will</u> result in a marriage that exceeds all of your greatest hopes for happiness and <u>will</u> last the rest of your life. In the succeeding chapters, I've hopefully explained what that principle is, why it works and some indication of what it takes to apply it to your life. Applying this principle to your own situation requires thought, honesty, effort and discipline on your part, but if you keep the underlying principle in mind, it will point the way and the results are certain.

I would like to close this book by showing how the principle answers the mystery questions above and reiterate how to avoid some of the obvious pitfalls to marriage by applying it.

WHO IS THE RIGHT PERSON FOR ME AND HOW WILL I KNOW?

The key principle is two people must willingly vowto do whatever is necessary to help the other personto become the best they can be. The good news is that you don't need to find some "one in a billion" soul mate for this to work, nearly any two people who share common values can do this and reap the rewards of a fantastic marriage. The problem is, you need to know who the other is well enough to know that you do share common values and be so impressed with this person that you <u>want</u> to dedicate the rest of your life to helping them. If both of these don't happen, you've probably picked the wrong person and it won't work.

There are a couple of common pitfalls in knowing the other person and determining if you have common values. One problem is that it takes time. You can't really get to know a person in days or even weeks. With lots of time together and great communication skills on both sides, it still takes months. Typically, it is much longer. You must see the person when they are not feeling well, when they are angry and when they are sad. You need to have discussed everything; friends, politics, religion, finances, sex, children, relatives and expectations on all of these in the future. There can be no "out of bounds" subjects.

If you have only recently "fallen in love", finding out who that other person really is, is more difficult. That same dopamine that is giving you that great euphoric feeling and causing you to want to be with them constantly, is also distorting your perception of them to a degree that is hard to believe if you haven't seen it in action in others. What can you do about it? First, recognize that your own perceptions may be distorted. Look for concrete examples of honesty and a willingness to help others that leave no room for doubt. Don't assume those traits are there because they must be, after all, this is such a great person! If you see examples to the contrary, don't be quick to write those times off as a mere misunderstanding, time after time. Even better, if you have a close friend or relative that you trust, ask them for their <u>honest</u> opinion promising to not hold it against them if they are contrary to your perception; this may be the most important thing they can ever do for you! Then listen to them, they are not under the influence of dopamine!

When it comes to shared common values; recognize that many of your values, as to what is important in life, come from your family of origin. Family size, family values, socio-economic background and religion can give a very different starting point. If you are going to commit your life to helping the other become the best that they can be, differing views of what that goal is, can make it more difficult. That is not to say that people from very different backgrounds shouldn't get married, it's just that even more communication is required because most people assume that others think like them and that can be a big mistake.

Also, you have to make sure that you are looking for the <u>right</u> values in a mate. If you are to help the other person grow, that requires the trust that only comes from <u>complete honesty</u>, a <u>willingness to help others</u> and <u>an openness to change.</u> How does the other person rate on these values? A good indication is how the <u>other</u> person treats their friends and others in this respect, because they may be on their "best behavior" with you. On the other hand, how important is how the person looks or how generous they are to you? Ask yourself this: what if they were in a bad accident leaving them terribly disfigured or were to experience financial ruin with little hope of recovery; would you still want to devote the rest of your life to them? If you hesitate, you may be looking for the wrong values. Enjoying how another person looks or what they can give to you can be a great plus, but not something to base a marriage on, as that can change overnight.

If you are already married, but not happy with it, the good news is you probably already know your mate fairly well. The bad news is that people can't change their basic personality and even have a hard time changing their behaviors and values. That having been said, discuss your unhappiness with your mate in a non-confrontational manner (i.e.; use "I feel . . ." rather than "You do . . ." accusations). If you come to the conclusion that <u>both</u> of you want a great marriage and are willing to live by the other-centered love principle, and are <u>both</u> willing to change if necessary, the upward spiral can start immediately. It will require a lot of communication and honest openness but it will work. If on the other hand, your mate is not willing to do this, even with the assistance of a marriage councilor, then you have to make the decision to accept the current situation as is (as a result of a previous bad decision to marry this person), or move on.

CAN I REALLY EXPECT TO LIVE HAPPILY EVER AFTER?

This is actually a two part question; will you be happy and how long will it last? As far as the happiness goes, it was explained in Chapter 7 that helping your partner to grow to be the best that they can be, will result in more happiness more frequently than any other worldly source of happiness. So there should be no doubt that a great marriage will bring great happiness.

As far as how long will it last; will I wake up some day and find that the spiral has collapsed? Absolutely not! In fact the question doesn't even make any sense! If the basis of your marriage, love, is a <u>decision</u> to do so, the only way for it to fail is to <u>decide</u> that you will <u>not</u> love. While that is possible, if it is the greatest source of happiness and fulfillment that you have ever known, deciding not to, is not likely. You can be completely certain that the marriage will not only last, but continue to grow as long as you live because neither you nor your spouse would ever decide that either of you should not have happiness and fulfillment.

Where the pitfall may come in, is the <u>unconscious</u> decision to stop loving. This happens when one person starts to act self centered, rather than other-centered, in areas that are detrimental to the other. Since you have already openly and directly discussed your mutual vows to be "other-centered", pointing out in a non-confrontational way that you feel hurt by something that happened, should illicit a positive response

44

from your partner. The resulting conversation will tend to clarify what was really going on in each person's mind and point the way to avoid the problem in the future. Such incidences will strengthen the marriage relationship and reinforce the promise to help each other. The key is constant and open communication. Good communication needs to happen every day because if it doesn't, the pressure of everyday life; earning a living, raising a family, etc., will skew your priorities. Problems not communicated will fester and grow until they threaten the relationship. I've found a 30 minute walk together every day will do wonders for your health and your marriage.

As discussed previously, the biggest pitfall you may ever have to face is an incident of unfaithfulness. This betrayal of trust that the other person is always looking out for your best interest, cuts so deep that it will take years to even get back to your starting point of trust. Without trust, there can be no spiral of happiness and growth. Unfortunately, people do make mistakes and when this happens, the best scenario is to forgive, learn from it so that it never happens again, reaffirm your intent to live up to your vows and start over. If it ever happens again, I would conclude that the person is not willing or capable of participating in the other-centered marriage spiral.

So in conclusion, if you want one of those rare marriages in which the people are really happily married forever, there is no luck involved. All you need is two people who understand the true meaning of love and decide to do so. It will take time to build the necessary trust, but love is patient. There will be setbacks, but love can endure all things. If you want it, it's yours. The results are certain.

So be it.

www.ingramcontent.com/pod-product-compliance
Lightning Source LLC
Chambersburg PA
CBHW051244120626
46547CB00014B/1786